Institiúid Te
Cork Institute of Technology

Bachelor of Engineering in Civil Engineering

Contaminated Land And Remediation

Cork South Docklands

Liam Lynch
Supervisor:
Claire McCarthy
Norma Hurley

May 2009

Acknowledgements

We wish to thank everyone who gave us help or
encouragement while we were working on this project. We
would especially like to thank the following: our project
supervisor Norma Hurley, lecturer John J. Murphy who
arranged for us to attend the Engineers Ireland Seminar,
Engineers Ireland, the engineer from Virtase FLI who
discussed remediation techniques with us, Olivia Holmes
from Arup Consulting Engineers who gave us information
and advice and Clwyd Evans for his direction and advice.

Executive Summary

The redevelopment of the Cork Docklands has a vital role in the revitalisation of Cork City Centre. The Cork Docklands Development Strategy identified the potential for contamination in this area. This project studies how the issue of contaminated land is currently addressed and recommends improvements to this approach. The South Docklands redevelopment is a key component of our study, it was used as a typical example of Brownfield development.

The study of the South Dockland site as a whole found that it was a dilapidated and almost idle area with the potential for 99 hectares of development. The industrial past of the area resulted in widespread contamination, generally in the fill layer. Oil contamination was found over much of the site but it is more a nuisance than a risk to human heath or the environment. Risks arise however from the presence of Vinyl Chloride and Dichloroethene. The four areas significantly contaminated by these substances require treatment or removal.

The history of remediation was investigated and the legislation relating to contaminated land was researched. It was found that in Ireland contaminated land tends to be sent to landfill or if not suited for landfill it is exported. The South Docklands redevelopment is an opportunity to pilot good practice in dealing with the contamination issue by treating the soil in Ireland. Irish legislation is found lacking when it comes to contaminated land, especially when compared to the UK. Our legislation only deals with the issue when the disposal or removal of waste is concerned or waters are being polluted.

Research of remediation techniques found there are several methods available these include: Dig and Dump, Containment methods, Pump and Treat, Thermal Absorption, Stabilisation/Solidification, Soil Washing and Bioremediation with Air Sparging.

From the research, it was concluded that the issue of contamination in the South Docklands is a substantial issue, the majority of this however is not a risk to human health or the environment. Also it was found that Ireland lacks relevant legislation for contaminated land and has a history of exporting contaminated soil or using containment methods, which is a short-term solution and may hinder redevelopment of a site in the future.

The following are some recommendations for the management of contaminated land and some specific recommendations to the Cork Docklands:

- **Introduction of a statutory definition and related legislation for contaminated land.**
- **Where possible a sustainable approach should be taken.**

- Remediation should be encouraged, by incentives for development on Brownfield sites or government grants for remediation projects.
- Raise public awareness to the advantages of Brownfield Remediation.
- Carry out detailed site specific soil and groundwater investigations.
- Treat areas of contamination where there is a hazardous link to end users of the site.
- Remediation should be carried out within the state using appropriate treatments that minimise waste and negative environmental effects.

1.0 Introduction

The Cork Docklands Project is a very large redevelopment project. The area was previously an industrial intensive area. Today there is still some commercial activity, however the South Docklands is to be converted into a mixed use, commercial and residential, urban area. Some proposals for the redevelopment are currently progressing through the various planning stages. The project presents many difficult challenges to its developers. One of these challenges is the remediation of contaminated soil and groundwater. This report aims to assess all of the various aspects of soil remediation with particular respect to the Cork South Docklands. A consideration of how countries which are highly progressive in the development of soil remediation, will afford us an education of how Ireland can aim to catch up with the best international standards. The report aims to give conclusions and personal recommendations for successful remediation of soil contamination in the South Docklands, in line with the best modern standards

With respect to the remediation of contaminated soil in the Cork Docklands, this report will outline the need for remediation, assess the scale of contamination through studies and discuss relevant legislation in Ireland and guidelines from other countries. The risk of contaminated soil to human health and the environment is also considered. The report also takes into account the different preferred practices with soil remediation in the U.K. compared with Ireland, including case studies.

A range of remediation solution are explained within the report to better illustrate their appropriateness to the Cork South Docklands. The future of remediation is anticipated with the use of sustainable and green practices.

Having gained a relevant knowledge of soil contamination and composition in the Cork South Docklands, reviewing the best remediation practices abroad and assessing Irish legislation and facilities we will outline our recommendations.

These recommendations will be for the improvement of remediation nationally and more specifically for the Cork Docklands. They will include amongst other recommendations, our recommended remediation procedures for the Cork South Docklands, legislation, guidelines, levels and types of contaminants worthy of treatment.

2.0 Plans for the Cork Docklands & its Soil Remediation Challenge.

In this chapter the plan for Corks South Docklands is revealed. The magnitude and necessity of the project are discussed as well as some of the plans proposed by developers.

The soil remediation challenge is also discussed in this chapter. The reason why contamination is a problem is explained, as well as the geology of the site. We also discuss why the soil remediation challenge is an opportunity for Ireland to adopt remediation correctly.

2.1 Development Overview

2.1.1 The Need for Development.

At the heart of the development for Cork City's future, is the redevelopment of the Cork Docklands. As time moves on, we see that in most of the developed world's big port cities, the inner city docks become less important for trade than areas further downstream, where more room is available for dock activity. This results in some parts of inner city docks becoming dilapidated and idle, which leaves the land readily available for development as an expansion of the city centre, such as the Irish Financial Services Centre (I.F.S.C.) in Dublin. Cork is no different in this regard, whilst there is still a lot of activity on the docks it is more practical to move this activity further afield to places like Ringaskiddy and use the inner docks for more valuable, area intensive development projects, such as offices and apartments. Redevelopment of the large area that is the south docklands leaves vast scope to expand the city centre in a planned modern fashion.

2.1.2 The South Docklands Site.

Fig 2.1 Outline of south docklands development area.
(www.corkdocklands.ie).

Our project will focus on the South Docklands. The South Docklands includes 99 hectares of development land as seen in fig 2.1 above. This area also includes four km of quay wall and 33ha of parkland (Coghlan et al, 2009). It is a massive development opportunity for cork city and one earmarked to go ahead in national and local development plans over the next twenty years. In 2007 the docklands development forum was set up by the government to watch over and speed up the development.

The site at the moment is generally commercially active in the western side whereas the eastern side is given over to amenities such as the Cork Show Grounds and Cork G.A.A. head quarters Páirc Uí Chaoimh. However some parts of the old Ford and Dunlop factories are still lying idle since their closure. This makes it a lot easier to begin development.

The Western side of the docks is home to large scale dock activity. Food and grain industries such as Odlums and R&H halls grain stores, have large facilities here. Gouldings Fertilizer also has a large facility, as well as oil giant Topaz and the E.S.B. generating station, (see fig 2.2).

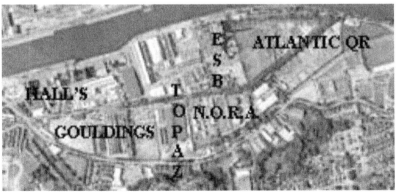

Fig 2.2 Location of sites.

2.1.3 The Vision.

The South Docklands is planned to be a mixed use urban site, with the potential for 25,000 residents and 27,000 jobs (coghlan et al, 2009). Fig 2.3 below portrays the vision of the south docklands at its fully developed stage.

Fig 2.3 Vision of Cork's South Docklands. (www.archiseek.com).

Some planning applications are already in place for developments such as the Atlantic Quarter, by Howard Holdings which has just been approved, in the Marina Precinct, where ford's old motor distribution centre was. This billion Euro development includes three tower blocks, 550,000 sq.ft. of office space, a 120,000 sq.ft. Conference centre, 575 residential units, a swing bridge over the Lee and much more (see Fig 2.4) (Howard Holdings plc, 2008).

Other big sites include I.A.W.S's large quay side site and Gouldings's slightly more inland site. I.A.W.S have submitted an a planning application for their 1.55Ha site where they propose the demolition of their R&H Halls grain silo's and the construction of 26,000 sq meters of office space and 165 residential units as well as retail outlets (Cork Docklands, 2008)

Fig 2.4 Artists impression of the proposed Atlantic Quarter. (www.myhome.ie).

If the development is completed, the outcome would be the equivalent of adding a town to the middle of the city. The sheer scale of the development would formulate the growth of Cork City to a modern and sophisticated level and help progress the city into the future.

2.2 Soil Remediation Challenge.

2.2.1 Corks South Docklands Situation.

With such a huge development in the pipeline for Cork's docklands, there are undoubtedly some soil issues to be faced. A major one of these is soil remediation. Much of the south docklands can be classified as what's known as a Brownfield site. This relates to area's with a previous industrial use which are abandoned or underused, and usually hold some form of contamination. Many of these sites can be found in the docklands, for example, Goulding's fertilizers, Fords old factory (Atlantic Quarter), Dunlop's factory, shell (Topaz) Ireland depot, and the National Oil Reserves Agency (N.O.R.A), see Fig 2.2. Many of which are designated as SEVESO sites which means that certain planning constraints apply with regard to population density, living in the vicinity, (Cork Docklands, 2008). The Scale of contamination is outlined in chapter 3 "Contamination in the South Docklands".

2.2.2 Why Contamination is a Problem.

Soil contamination has become more recognized globally as a health and environmental hazard in recent times. Society has become more environmentally aware in the past few decades and the origins of certain human illnesses can be linked with harmful substances that can be found in contaminated soil. This is why it is imperative that hazardous contaminated soil does not have any contact with people and the environment around them as it can not only directly affect their health but also indirectly through the water they drink or the vegetables they could grow, etc. Cancer causing Carcinogens can be found in the contaminated soil as well as contaminants known as Perchloroethylenes also known as PCE's which are linked to very negative neurological effects on humans.

The link between the contaminated soil and the surrounding environment must be cut off, we can do this by containing it and covering it over or have the soil removed to a secured landfill or even better, treat it once and for all through the vast array of processes and new technologies that have become available.

Some of the contaminants act as a catalyst for the degradation of concrete and other building materials.

2.2.3 An Opportunity for Ireland to deal correctly with such a challenge.

The development on the docklands is an opportunity for Ireland to try and remediate the soil in a sustainable fashion. Brownfield sites are sites which have previously been developed and may hold contaminants. In a country with a sparse industrial past, Brownfield sites are not very common. Usually in cases like this the soil is simply exported to countries like Germany and Holland where they have a longer tradition of soil treatment and the facilities to do so. If Cork could adopt some of the treatment techniques in use in other European countries and use them to remediate the soil, perhaps we would become more confident in our ability to deal with this problem and keep the money used to treat the soil in the local economy.

There are many aspects of legislation from the E.U and the Irish government which constrain development on such contaminated lands, however no major principle soil remediation laws are in place as yet, this will be discussed in chapter 4 later. However the challenge faced by the cork docklands, to deal correctly with the soil remediation is an important issue, and must be dealt with before any actual development occurs.

Due to the large extent of Brownfield sites in the south docklands, the necessity for proper legislation on contaminated soil has become apparent. The development of corks docklands affords the governing bodies a good opportunity to develop proper legislation on the issue.

2.2.4 Cork Docklands Soil Geology.

The general makeup of the South docklands soil geology, in descending order is shown in table 1.

A,	0.2m of pavement
B,	0.5 – 4m of Fill, containing clay and rubble
C,	3-5 m of Clay
D,	up to 25m of a gravel aquifer

Table 2-1: **The general geological composition of south docklands.** (O'Connor, 2007).

Other Soil and Geology investigations, such as that of the Atlantic Quarter and the Halls site give similar findings. However I.A.W.S's Halls site, (on the western side of the south dock's) has a much shallower clay layer of 0.7m – 2.2m (Origin Enterprises, 2008). The clay layer acts as a barrier for the aquifer, in that it is a good substance for blocking the path of contaminants into the aquifer. But as a shallow clay layer is not very effective, contamination has infiltrated the aquifer in this location and similar locations throughout the south docklands.

The shape of the south docklands in its current form dates back to the early 1800's when the harbour was dredged and the south docks were reclaimed and raised. This explains the layer of fill that covers most of the area. Below this is a clay layer of varying depths and then a layer of gravel and some sands. The sands and gravels can be attributed to deposits from glaciation. Aquifers are mainly present in the gravel strata, there are also various perched aquifers throughout the site.

Due to the effect of the tidal currents and the large risk of flooding, raising ground levels has been a consideration of some of the planning. This would change the composition of the geology near the surface. It is also a good way of cutting off some of the direst connection between contaminated land and the people above.

At design stage it is very important to consider the sites soil geology, as it presents the challenge required to build adequate foundations for proposed buildings.

3.0   Contamination in the South Docklands

This chapter outlines the findings from contamination studies and Environmental Impact Statements carried out on the South Docklands.

3.1   South Docklands Contamination Study

As the South Docklands had a number of industrial uses over the last century, DHV and T.J. O'Connor & Associates were appointed by Cork County Council to undertake a contamination study in the South Docklands to identify any contamination of soil or groundwater. The objectives of the study were to identify contamination sources and to obtain an estimation of the extent of contamination. Figure 3.1 below indicates areas of contamination encountered during the study.

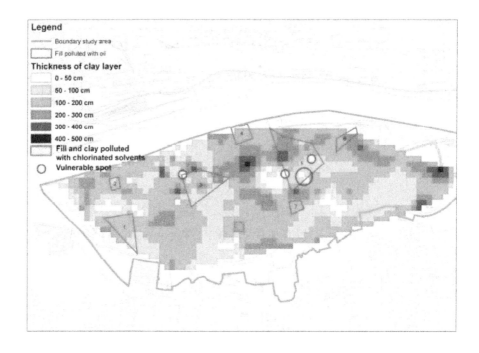

Figure 3.1: Presence of contamination,

(O' Connor, 2007).

3.1.1 Methodology.

Strata Survey was contracted to carry out the site investigation in the South Docklands. This investigation involved; 91 monitoring wells (generally 6m), 1 well (30m), 1 well (20m), 1 well (13m, bedrock hit where intention was to install well 30m bgl), 3 wells (10m), 244 trial pits (2m), groundwater samples, soil samples and sediment samples from watercourses and the Atlantic Pond, (O' Connor, 2007).

Activities included in the conservation study were the collection and analysis of soil samples, the completion of groundwater flow and contaminant transport models and the assessment of biodegradation of organic pollutants in the groundwater. The laboratory results obtained were compared to the Dutch List Values. A computer model called Sanscrit was used to assess the urgency of remediation. The model determines whether a case has the potential to "cause unacceptable risks for human, ecosystem or transport of contamination via groundwater".

3.1.2 Overview of Results.

The fill layer in the Docklands was found to contain a variety of contaminants. Many of which were above Dutch Intervention Values (D.H.V.'s). This fill was used to raise the ground many years ago while expanding the docklands to its current shape. The contamination is believed to be a result of level rising with contaminated material and also by the land use in the area, such as car manufacture and fuel storage.These contaminants include; lead, copper, zinc, arsenic, cadmium, mercury, polcyclic aromatics (PAH), mineral oil, (O' Connor, 2007).

Oil (hydrocarbon) contamination in the South Docklands is estimated to be 105,000m³ located in seven zones over 8 hectares (O'Connor, 2007). The human health risk as a result is limited because there were not poisonous derivatives found. For gardens or open space the presence of oil contamination would be a nuisance. A thick clay layer protects the aquifer from the spreading of the contamination. Where the clay layer is thin or perforated it should be replaced or repaired to continue to provide protection to the aquifer.

The other main contaminants include mobile volatile chlorinated hydrocarbons (VCH's), estimated at 26,000 m3 and non-mobile heavy metals. Four areas where VCH's are found to be greater than the Dutch Intervention Values have been identifies throughout the South Docklands, at the Ford distribution centre, the Marina, at the National Oil Reserves Agency (NORA) and the boundary of Topaz and Free Foam Plastics (O'Connor, 2007). These spots are identified in Figure 3.1 above.

The action to be undertaken is not necessarily to remediate all the contamination found in the South Docklands. This would be impractical and not very cost effective. Before any work begins on site, careful consideration should be made in relation to whether remediation steps need to be carried out or if the contamination is to be left in place. If the decision is to leave the contamination in place the land user or local authority must have an adequate attitude when it comes to the future land use and whether any steps should be taken to protect the surrounding soil or groundwater in the area.

3.1.3 Groundwater Flow and Transport Modelling.

As part of the study a three-dimensional finite difference groundwater flow model and a RT3D transport model were carried out. It was carried out in order to simulate stationary groundwater flow and VCH transport. In the study area within the South Docklands four species of VCH were assessed perchloroethene (PCE), trichloroethene (TCE), dichloroethene (DCE) and vinyl chloride (VC). Neither PCE nor TCE were measured in excess of Dutch Halfway Values. Therefore only DCE and VC concentrations were further assessed.

The three remediation options in the model primarily involve the excavation of the core sites of DCE and VC pollution from the clay layer. The removal of the core spots of DCE and VC pollution would immediately reduce the DCE concentrations below DIV. Figure 3.2 below illustrates these core spots.

The model shows that stimulation of biodegradation would reduce to one year the time for the concentrations of DCE and VC in the aquifer to fall below DIV. This is achieved by injecting nutrients into the groundwater. This is the fastest but most expensive remediation. Combining excavation with pump and treat again allows for the speeding up of the groundwater remediation. Pumping wells are installed and the water is treated before being discharged. The method most likely to be undertaken would simply be the excavation of the core areas of pollution. It would be faster than leaving nature to take its course and involve reasonably acceptable costs.

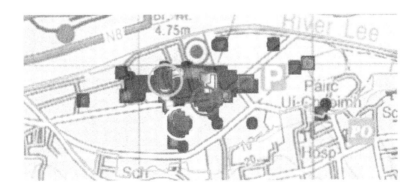

Figure 3.2: Circles indicate the location of the core sites of DCE and VC pollution. (This figure shows the VC concentrations in the clay after half a year of low breakdown scenario), (O'Connor, 2007).

3.2 Environmental Impact Statements

Although the country is currently in an economic downturn the planned redevelopment of the South Docklands has not come to a stand still. There are a number of developments in the planning process or have received planning permission. For example at the end of March the proposed development of the Atlantic Quarter was successful in achieving planning permission from Cork City Council. As part of the planning process an Environmental Impact Statement is completed and within this the subject of excavated material is partially addressed. The following paragraphs contain information obtained from Environmental Impact Statements for the Atlantic Quarter and the Port Quarter developments.

3.2.1 Atlantic Quarter.

Fig 3.3 Atlantic Quarter Site. (www.independent.ie).

The proposed Atlantic Quarter development is to include a basement car park, of which the lowest level will be approximately 6 metres below existing ground level. As a result of this basement, the site preparation will involve the excavation of material covering the entire footprint of the site. This equates to approximately 275,000 m^3 of soil, (Howard Holdings plc, 2008). From initial soil samples taken from the site it was determined that this excavated soil would require disposal in a variety of different locations. This was because a proportion of the soil was found to contain varying quantities and varieties of chemicals. Figure 3.4 shown below indicates the site within the South Docklands and Figure 3.3 shows a picture of the site.

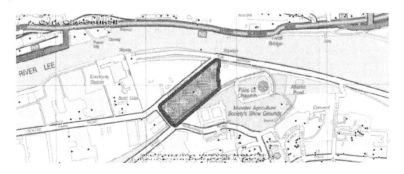

Figure 3.4: Atlantic Quarter site
(www.planenquiry.corkcity.ie)

In order to plan appropriately for the disposal of material, four categories were established which the material would be classified under. Volumes were calculated from a preliminary investigation and were used to estimate the quantities of material that would be assigned to each category. These figures are displayed in Table 3.3 below.

Classification	Material Type	Volume of material (m³)
Category A	Inert waste -Permitted site -Sum of 6 PAHs < 2 mg/kg	99,040.37
Category B	Inert waste -Suitable for Inert Landfill -Sum of 6 PAHs > 2 mg/kg & Sum of 17 PAHs < 100 mg/kg	22,353.50
Category C	Non hazardous waste -Non hazardous waste acceptable at landfills in Ireland for non hazardous waste -Sum of 10 PAHs < 40 mg/kg	136,992.37
Category D	Non hazardous waste -No accepting facilities in Ireland i.e. Export -Sum 10 PAHs > 40 mg/kg	11,964.75
	Total Volume	270,350.99

3.2.2 Port Quarter.

This is a mixed-use development at the R&H Hall's Site in the South Docklands. The location of the site within the South Docklands is shown in figure 3.5. As with the Atlantic Quarter development, the plans for this site include the building of a two-storey basement with a capacity for 413 cars and storage space. The material to be removed from the site during the construction process was categorised in the same way as for the Atlantic Quarter. This is displayed in Table 3.5 below.

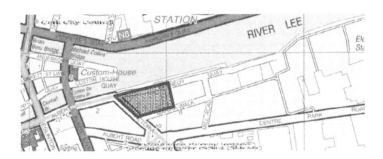

Figure 3.5: Port Quarter site.
(www.planenquiry.corkcity.ie).

Classification	Material Type	Volume of material (m^3)
Category A	Inert waste -Permitted site -Sum of 6 PAHs < 2 mg/kg	17,217
Category B	Inert waste -Suitable for Inert Landfill -Sum of 6 PAHs > 2 mg/kg & Sum of 17 PAHs < 100 mg/kg	2,472
Category C	Non hazardous waste -Non hazardous waste acceptable at landfills in Ireland for non hazardous waste -Sum of 10 PAHs < 40 mg/kg	26,432
Category D	Non hazardous waste -No accepting facilities in Ireland i.e. Export -Sum 10 PAHs > 40 mg/kg	19,455
	Total Volume	65,576.00

Table 3.4: Categories of excavated material, (Origin Enterprises, 2008).

3.2.3 Discussion.

In both Environmental Impact Statements the author describes each category of waste in three ways, firstly whether it is inert or non-hazardous, secondly the type of facility it is destined for and finally it's PAH range. In spite of this detail the reader is still a little in the dark as to the quality of the soil. According to the Environmental Protection Agency inert waste is defined as "waste that does not undergo any significant physical, chemical or biological transformations." It is not likely to result in environmental or human health risk. (EPA, 2007) They do not have a specific definition of non-hazardous waste but a definition is available for hazardous waste, which states that the waste "is so classified because it displays properties that make it hazardous to human health or the environment." (EPA, 2007)

These definitions combined with the Figures from the Dutch Standards which state that for a sum of 10 PAH the Dutch target value is 1mg/kg and the Dutch intervention value is 40mg/kg it is understood that non-hazardous waste is contaminated material. However this material is believed not to have the potential for environmental or human health risk. It must be still be disposed of in appropriate sites such as landfills licensed to take such PAH concentrations or exported to facilities with the appropriate remediation technology.

4.43% of the material to be excavated from the Atlantic Quarter site and 29.67% material from the Port Quarter site will require export as there is no facility available in Ireland to accept this material. This will have a significant effect on the costs at the initial stage of both projects. The disposal of waste in general from both projects will involve careful planning, as there are four categories of waste with four different destinations for each. Initially the excavated material will have to be segregated on site into the correct categories. A traffic management plan will need to be developed to ensure the least disturbance to surrounding businesses and residences and a timetable produced for the extraction of the different waste categories from site to coincide with the traffic management plan and exporting schedule.

4.0 Legislation and Guidelines

This chapter outlines the legislative situation in Ireland and the UK when contaminated soil is encountered. In relation to the legislation, the identification of when contaminated soil becomes waste is also stated. Finally land-use planning guidelines are explained and an example of such guidelines is provided for the Goulding Chemicals Ltd site in the South Docklands.

4.1 Contaminated land in Ireland

In Ireland at present there are no specific guidelines or regulations in place to deal with contaminated soil or land. This is due to the misconception that Ireland does not have a problem with historic contamination of soil. In fact a study conducted by the EPA in 1998 found that there is approximately 2,371 sites in Ireland, which have the potential to pose a risk to soil or groundwater. (Heffernan, 2008) This is minimal when compared to the UK where it is estimated between 5,000 and 20,000 problem sites exist. (Motherway, 2009) But with the growth of redevelopment of sites especially in city areas and dockland sites there is the potential for growth in these numbers. A growing number of contaminated sites would call for a procedure to deal with land with contaminated soil.

4.1.1 The Role of the EPA

The Environmental Protection Agency is an organisation that deals with the implementation of environmental policy in Ireland. The Agency has no power to make policy but has the power to enforce licenses and to take action to prosecute those not in compliance. The EPA sets targets for the clean up of sites and is a source of information and advice. Although Ireland has no guidelines or legislation dealing specifically with contaminated land some of the legislation and polices already enforced by the EPA can be applied to contaminated land.

4.1.2 Waste Management Act 1996-2008 – Waste Licensing

The Waste Management Act becomes applicable to contaminated soil when activities identified in the Third and Fourth Schedules of the Act are to be undertaken. An example of such an activity is "land treatment, including biodegradation of liquid or sludge discards in soils". (Waste Management Act 1996-2008, 1996) These activities require a waste licence that is issued by the EPA on the conclusion that there is no evidence the activity will cause environmental pollution.

4.1.3 Local Government (Water Pollution) Acts

One role of a local authority is to "prevent or control pollution of waters". (Local Government (Water Pollution) Act 1977, 1977) Under the Water Pollution Act where a local authority finds it to be necessary a local authority may serve written notice to anybody owning or in control of polluting matter on a premises. This notice shall include measures to prevent polluting matter entering water, direct the receiver of the notice to undertake these actions and provides a time period to complete the task.

4.2 Waste or not waste

As Ireland is a legislative vacuum when it comes to contaminated land often Irish legislation does not come into effect unless a quantity of 'waste' is involved. Therefore it is important that where contaminated soil is concerned, what qualifies as 'waste' is clearly identifiable. A new Waste Framework Directive is currently being introduced in Europe; this will affect the definition of waste. The current and future situation is dealt with below under the headings of the VWalle case and the new Waste Framework Directive.

4.2.1 Van de Walle Case

The current definition of when contaminated soil becomes waste ids based on the precedent set by the European Court of Justice (ECJ) ruling on the Van de Walle case. This case arose as a result of leakage from a petrol station storage tank in Belgium. The case was related to the offence of abandoning waste; therefore the identification of what constituted waste or not was an important issue. The definition of waste was given much consideration as it given in Article 1 of the Waste Framework Directive 75/442/EEC where it states that waste is "any substance or object in the categories set out in Annex 1 which the holder discards or intends or is required to discard". After studying the legislation and the potential for human health risk the EJC achieved a decision. "The decision was achieved by interpreting the verb 'to discard'". (Cox, 2005) It was interpreted that the spillage of the petrol was accidental was 'discarded'.

The ruling stated that "an accidental spillage of hydrocarbons and the soil contaminated by the spillage constituted waste for the purposes of the EU Framework Directive 75/442/EEC". (Heffernan, 2008) This means that even the unexcavated soil is considered waste. Prior to this case the soil, if left in place as part of the ground it was not considered waste.

4.2.2 The new Waste Framework Directive

The new Directive 2008/98/EC clarifies EU legislation on waste and "replaces the existing Waste Framework Directive, the Hazardous Waste Directive and the Waste Oil Directive." (Association for Organics Recycling, 2008) One of the key points of the directive was "the clarification of the distinction between waste and non-waste". (Euroalert.net, 2008) Some materials categorised as waste in current directives will no longer be waste. Among these materials is "land (in situ) including unexcavated contaminated soil and buildings permanently connected with land". (Waste Framework Directive 2008/98/EC, 2008) This change in policy nullifies the EJC Van de Walle case precedent.

Also the new directive further defines the polluter pays principle stating "The polluter-pays principle is a guiding principle at European and international levels, and therefore, the waste producer and the waste holder should manage the waste in a way that guarantees a high level of protection of the environment and human health." (Euroalert.net, 2008) This ensures that the land is maintained at or returned to a satisfactory level. This new directive was brought into force on 12 December 2008 and all EU member states must adjust their laws and regulations to comply with the directive by 12 December 2010.

4.3 Contaminated land in the U.K.

In the UK there is a clear regulatory framework for the management of contaminated land. This is stated in the Contaminated Land Regime which is contained in Part IIA of the Environmental Protection Act, 1990. Within this document a statutory definition of contaminated land is provided along with a framework for the identification and remediation of contaminated land.

4.3.1 Legal definition

Part IIA of the Environmental Protection Act, 1990 defines "contaminated land" as "any land which appears to the local authority in whose area the land is situated to be in such a condition, by reason of substances in, on or under the land, that (a) significant harm is being caused or there is a significant possibility of such harm being caused; or (b) pollution of controlled waters is being, or is likely to be, caused" (defra, 2008)

4.3.2 Contaminated Land Regime

A regime for identifying and remediating contaminated land was established in the UK by the Environment act 1995. This act inserted Part IIA into the existing Environmental Protection Act 1990. Further regulations and guidelines also back this legislation.

The legislation is used when the contamination is proven to be "causing unacceptable risk to human health or the wider environment", (Forest-heath.gov.uk, 2007). The standard that the legislation operates under is that the land should be 'suitable for use', as a result not all contaminated land is covered by this Act. Remedial works are assessed in relation to three factors, firstly the intensity of the contamination present, secondly the extent of it and finally the end use which the site is intended for. A site is deemed to be contaminated when the local authority has established that a complete source pathway receptor linkage exists. The statutory definition stated in Paragraph 4.3.1 is then applicable to the land.

If a local authority believes a site is possibly contaminated they may need to carry out a site investigation. By doing so they establish whether a complete source pathway receptor linkage exists and therefore identify under the statutory definition that the site is contaminated. Before the site investigation is carried out any people with an interest in the site must be notified. If there appears to be urgent reasons for the investigation to be carried out, such as "immediate risk of serious pollution of the environment or serious harm to human health", (Forest-heath.gov.uk, 2007) no notice can be given. On completion of the investigation a written document is produced, it contains the perceived source pathway receptor linkages and evidence of their existence. The enforcing body which carries out these activities is the local authority unless the site is designated a 'special site' such as land where water intended for water supply is is at risk or industries carrying out oil refining.

When land has been established as 'contaminated land' the person responsible for the clean up must be identified. There are two classes of responsibility, Class A which is in accordance with 'the polluter pays 'principle, the person who caused the pollution and Class B, the landowner or occupier of the land.

The Act also defines what remediation, it defines it as any actions undertaken to prevent, remedy or minimise the effects of contamination or the returning of land or waters to their original state. The local authority encourages voluntary remediation however if this is not a possibility then they shall serve a remediation notice on the person or persons deemed liable for the clean up. This notice will identify the remediation works that need to be carried out and a time limit to complete them by.
However when voluntary remediation is to be carried out, a remediation statement must be first submitted to the local authority. In this the remediation activities, details of the person who will carry out the works and an expected timeline must be included. This must be approved by the local authority or they will enforce their remediation plan on the liable person.

4.4 Analytical/assessment methods commonly used in Ireland

As Ireland does not have a legal standard for soil contamination methods used in the UK or in other EU countries are common practice. The method in use by Cork County Council as common policy has been the Dutch Standards.

4.4.1 Dutch Standards

The Dutch standards are soil quality standards providing threshold values for contaminants. These threshold values include a target value (DTV) which is the baseline concentration value below which compounds and/or elements are known or assumed not to affect the natural properties of the soil and an intervention value (DIV) is the maximum tolerable concentration above which remediation is required. This occurs if one or more compounds in concentrations equal to or higher than the intervention value is found in more than 25 m³ of soil or 1000 m³ of ground water.

Unlike other commonly used methods, these values allow for the contaminated soil to be brought to a level suitable for any use rather than for to a specific land use. The values are a concentration of a standard soil type. This standard is a soil of 10% organic matter and 25% clay. (Sanaterre, 2008) Therefore for a soil with different levels of organic matter and clay content, formulas are provided to adjust these values.

4.4.2 CLEA model

The Contaminated Land Exposure Assessment (CLEA) is a methodology to estimate the human health risk from contaminants in soil when exposed to it over a long period of time. In early 1990's research was started to develop a framework for assessing human health risks arising from land contamination. This research launched four Contaminated Land Reports and Soil Guideline Values (SGV) for individual substances. This method complies with Part IIA of the Environmental Protection Act 1990. The Contaminated Land Exposure Assessment CLEA model involves inputting, site characteristics, level of contamination, potential pathways and receptors to produce an output. The output is calculated in relation to contaminant concentration and the potential exposure of people living or working in the area. The Soil Guidance Values are derived by calculating the intake due to exposure with the Tolerable Daily Intake (TDI).

4.5 Land-use planning guidelines

The land-use planning guidelines provide advice for developers and landowners as to the suitability of a development in relation to the level of risk of a major incident occurring in the surrounding area.

4.5.1 PADHI – HSE' s Land Use Planning Methodology

The Planning Advice for Developments near Hazardous Installations (PADHI) – HSE's Land Use Planning Methodology is a document produced by the Health and Safety Executive (HSE). When a planning permission is sought for a development in the vicinity of a major hazard chemical installation or pipeline the local planning authority must consult the HSE. The HSE analyse the "consequences of a major accident at the hazardous installation" (HSE, 2003) and will then give their advice in the form of 'advise against' or 'don't advise against' granting planning permission. The PADHI document is often used by the planning authority to predict what the outcome of the HSE analysis might be.

The HSE assigns a consultation distance (CD) around the hazard installation. It then assesses the risks and their consequences should a major accident occur. In making their decision on a development the HSE considers two elements, firstly which zone it is in and secondly what sensitivity level is it categorised under. The zones are areas of the CD, which are at different levels of risk. The inner zone has the greatest risk attributed to it, as it is the closest to the hazard installation. The sensitivity levels are the types of potential development categorised into levels ranging from least vulnerable to most vulnerable if a major accident were to occur. These categories are listed in Table 4.1 that follows.

		People at work, parking
		Developments for use by the general public
		Developments for use by vulnerable people
		Very large and sensitive

	developments

Table 4.1: Sensitivity levels (HSE, 2003)

The decision making process involves using both the zone and the sensitivity level which apply to the proposed development and reading the answer from a decision matrix such as the one displayed below in Table 4.2. In this table DAA means Don't Advice Against development while AA stands for Advise Against development.

Level of Sensitivity	Development in Inner Zone	Development in Middle Zone	Development in Outer Zone
1	DAA	DAA	DAA
2	AA	DAA	DAA
3	AA	AA	DAA
4	AA	AA	AA

Table 4.2: Decision matrix (HSE, 2003)

4.5.2 Land-use Planning Advice for Cork City Council in relation to Goulding Chemicals Ltd. at Centre Park Road, Cork

This is an example of land-use planning advice for a specific hazard source, the Goulding Chemicals Ltd. Site. This document was produced by the HSA for Cork City Council to provide the planning authority with guidance with respect to what forms of development should and shouldn't be granted planning permission in the areas surrounding the site. The site is considered a "lower tier Seveso site under the European communities (Control of major accident hazards involving dangerous substances) Regulations. (Conneely, 2006).

A similar method to that laid out in the PADHI document was used. When completing the initial study a "potential major accident involving Ammonium Nitrate Fertiliser (ANF)"was considered. (Conneely, 2006). A consultation distance (CD) was established around the site and divided into zones of decreasing levels of risk as the distance from the hazard source increases. However the difference in this document is that the objective is not to assess the suitability of a particular development. The outcome of this report is to identify for each zone of the CD, what sensitivity level of development is acceptable within it. Figure 4.1 below indicates the three zones.

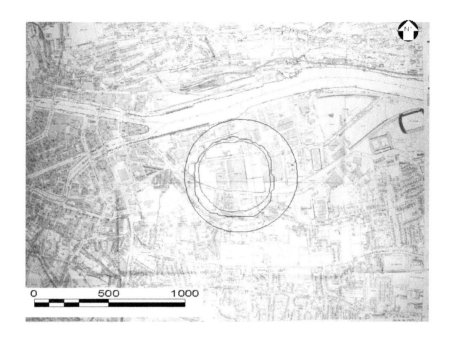

Fig 4.1: Risk Contours **(Conneely, 2006)**

The result of this study identified that the inner zone within the red boundary is not very suitable for development, advised only suitable for developments not frequently occupied such as a transformer station. The middle zone is less restricted, developments such as workplaces, small retail development and residential units of densities increasing as distance from red boundary line increases. The outer zone has no restrictions with the exception of sensitive developments such as hospitals and crèches. These developments require further consultation with the HSA. (Conneely, 2006)

5.0 Human Health or Environmental Risks

The following chapter provides a brief description of
the risk assessment method commonly used in
Ireland. The chapter also provides a brief insight into
the possible human health and environmental risks
found to be present in the South Docklands.

5.1   Risk Assessment

It is important to carry out a risk assessment on a site
of a proposed development as it must be assessed
whether the land is at present a human health or
environmental risk or if there is potential for risks to
arise from the development.

5.1.1 Definition

Risk assessment can be defined as "the formal process of identifying, assessing and evaluating the health [and environmental] risks that may be associated with a hazard" (Burden, 2009)

5.1.2   Risk Assessment

Currently in Ireland there is, as with the legislation, no established methodology for the determination of human health or environmental risk. At present the system in common use is the identification of Source Pathway Receptor (SPR) linkages with the aid of a conceptual site models (CSM). This involves the identification of the sources of contamination, the methods by which humans or the environment is exposed to it (such as via groundwater or direct contact) and the targets that will be affected by the contamination (for example residents or river). A conceptual model involves producing a visual interpretation of the site, including the relevant aspects such as location of water supply, water table, residential areas, sources of contamination etc. From this the possible pathways are identified and whether the targets are at risk or not can be examined. An example of this is shown in Figure 5.1. A target is only at risk of exposure to the contamination if all three, source-pathway-receptor are present.

Figure 5.1: Example of a conceptual model, (Musgrave, 2008)

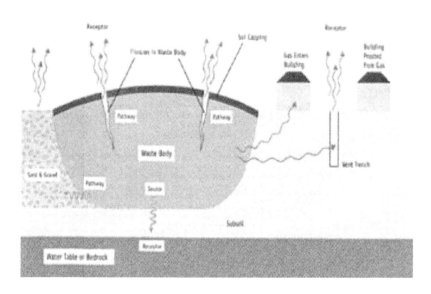

5.2 Human health or environmental risks in the South Docklands

The Contamination Study carried out by T.J. O'Connor provided an insight into the possible human health risk and environmental risk present in the South Docklands. The following paragraphs illustrate the findings of this report.

5.2.1 Human Health Risk

In general the risk to human health in the Docklands is due to the varying levels of contamination level in the fill layer. This gives rise to unpredictable possibilities of a risk to children who may come in direct contact with the fill material. Lead, PAH, vinyl chloride and 1,2-dichloroethene contamination has the potential to cause health risks in areas intended for leisure use, residential areas (with gardens and/or playground) and public spaces as a result.

The ESB site contains the contaminants vinyl chloride and 1,2-dichloroethene which will result in human health risk for land use for residential use (without garden and/or playground) and sites of work, industry, social or cultural venues. 1,2-dichloroethene also results in potential risks if the Shell site is developed for residential use (without garden and/or playground) or for office space. The same future lands uses are vulnerable to human health risks caused by the presence of vinyl chloride on the NORA site.

Vinyl chloride and 1,2-dichloroethene are degradation products of Perchloroethene (PCE) and Trichloroethene (TCE). The health risks involved with exposure to PCE are as a result of inhalation. Exposure to low concentrations of PCE gives rise to neurological symptoms such as dizziness, headaches, behavioural changes and sleepiness. Lifetime exposure to vinyl chloride at levels above 0.1mg/l may cause cancer.

Table 4.3 provides a general overview of the potential for human health risk in the South Docklands. It addresses each site individually with a number of possible future uses considered.

Landowner / plot	Future land use					
	RG	R-	PS	L	WIS	INF
IAWS 2	+	o	o	o	-	-
IAWS 3 / former Esso	+	u	u	u	u	-
IAWS 4	+	o	o	o	-	-
IAWS 5	-	-	-	-	-	-
IAWS 6	-	-	-	-	-	-
Odlums	+	-	-	-	-	-
Southern Milling	-	-	-	-	-	-
S-Tyres / Dineen Crash Repairs	+	o	+	+	-	-
Walsh Warehousing	-	-	-	-	-	-
Arkady Feed Ltd.	-	-	-	-	-	-
Colso	-	-	-	-	-	-
Marina Commercial Park	+	+	o	+	+	-
Irish Shell	+	+	-	+	+	-
National Oil Reserve	+	+	-	-	+	-
ESB	+	o	o	o	-	-
Tedcastle	+	-	+	+	-	-
Cork Warehouse Co.	+	-	-	-	-	-
Ford Vehicle Distribution Centre	+	+	o	o	-	-
GAA and the Showgrounds	+	-	+	+	-	-
Bord na Mona	-	-	-	-	-	-
J.W. Greene & Co.	-	-	-	-	-	-
O'Shea Leader	-	-	-	-	-	-
Main Port	-	-	-	-	-	-
Monahan's Road Industrial Park	-	-	-	-	-	-
Sheehan & Sullivan Coal Importers	-	-	-	-	-	-
Lane Development	-	-	-	-	-	-
Rehab Recycling	+	o	o	o	-	-
Scrap Metal Yard	-	-	-	-	-	-
Nat Ross Ltd.	-	-	-	-	-	-
Free Foam	+	o	o	o	-	-
J. Healy Ltd.	+	o	o	o	-	-
Atlantic Pond+connected ditches				-		
Ditches Tedcastle				+		

Legend
L — Leisure
RG — Residential with garden
R- — Residential without garden
PS — Public space
WIS — Work/industry/social activities
INF — Infrastructure
+ — health risks to be expected
o — health risks to be expeced only on playgrounds
- — no health risks to be expected

Table 5.3: Results of health risk assessment per site
(O'Connor, 2007)

5.2.2 Environmental risk

When assessing the risks to the flora and fauna the whole South Docklands area was considered. Assumptions were made in assessing the risks present such as that approximately 30% of the area with be used as open space including parks and gardens and the roots of trees and plants with be within 1 metre below ground level.

Lead and copper concentration levels within the top 1 metre below ground level have the potential to cause ecological problems. Also in "the ditches around Tedcastle's and along the northwest side of Ford Vehicle Distribution Centre and Cork Warehouses" the sediment quality is poor, and if the area were to be developed into a nature zone, ecological risks would be present.

6.0 History and Case Studies of Remediation in Ireland and the U.K.

It is important to understand the history of remediation and to review case studies when looking for solutions. The reason for this is that it helps to determine what best practice is and how we can learn from the past.

6.1 Remediation in Ireland.

6.1.1 Irelands Brownfield sites.

While Ireland's past was not very industrious, it still has its share of Brownfield sites.

The Environmental Protection Agency (EPA) has estimated that there are between 2000 and 2500 Brownfield sites in Ireland (Motherway, 2009). These sites include railway depots, old gasworks and mines, closed landfills, petrol stations, scrap yards, chemical industry sites and much more. It would be expected that the remediation of contaminated land will become a growing issue as our more recent booms of industry shut down and leave behind Brownfield sites. These sites need to be cleaned up to prevent movement of mobile contaminants into groundwater. Soil remediation is an issue that Ireland is only learning to deal with recently. There is a larger pressure from environmental authorities to remediate contaminated sites these days than ever before. A lot of new Brownfield sites have come on stream during the last decade as the building boom took place. Large sites such as the former Irish steel site on Haulbowline Island (Fig 6.1) and the Cork and Dublin docklands are examples of this.

Fig 6.1 Irish Steel site on Haulbowline Island, Cork.
(www.passagewestmonkstown.ie).

6.1.2 Irish Best Practice.

Ireland has taken the remediation of contaminated soil much more seriously in the last decade than ever before. Irish Legislation does not have a definition for what land is considered contaminated / Brownfield (Motherway, 2009). When it comes to dealing with soil contamination, Ireland tends to draw on snippets of other legislation which is already in place, mainly the Waste Management Act 1996-2008. The act states that contaminated soil should be disposed of by a licensed contractor (ENVA, 2008). Previous to this most soil of a highly contaminated nature was dumped in a landfill without being treated. Ireland does not have the facilities to deal with large quantities of hazardous waste soil. Instead we tend to export our soil to other countries to deal with. In Ireland in 2006, there was over 400,000T of contaminated material exported from development locations, instead of being treated on site (Piddington, 2009).

In 2006, 284,184 tonnes of hazardous waste was generated in Ireland and of this 48% was exported (FinFacts, 2007). Fig 6.2 below portrays the breakdown of where this material was treated.

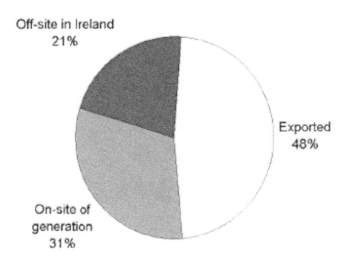

Fig 6.2Area of treatment of hazardous soil in Ireland in 2006. (www.finfacts.com).

It is better to be able to treat contaminated soil on site as it reduces costs and is a more sustainable solution as the soil can be reused. Ireland should vastly reduce its exports and begin to deal with its own hazardous waste. Hopefully in the future, Ireland's best practice for soil remediation would be to become more self sufficient and sustainable.

Risk assessment of contaminated soil is borrowed from the Dutch Intervention Values. Ireland does not yet have any proper methodology to assess the health risks to humans from contaminated soil.

An Environmental Protection Agency license is required if more than 5000 Tonnes of contaminated material is required to be removed off site. If there is less than 5000 Tones to be removed a Local Authority Permit is required. This is another reason why on site remediation is better practice.

The primary onus of payment, for a sites remediation process in Ireland, is firstly on the polluter, and then on the land owner. If either of these is not found the onus falls on the taxpayer.

6.2 Irish Soil Remediation Case Studies

6.2.1 Sir John Rogerson' s Quay, Dublin.

The remediation of the former gasworks site at Rogersons Quay in Dublin (see Fig 6.3 below) was perhaps the most similar project to the one faced by Cork docklands. The site is just under 9 hectares in size and like Cork Docklands was to become a mixed use site. The land is adjacent to the river Liffey and due to the level of contaminants found, it had to be remediated, (Brown at al, 2006). Interestingly the site required not one but two Waste Management Licenses. These were the first such license to be issued with regards to contaminated land in Ireland.

Fig 6.3 Sir John Rogerson's Quay Site, Dublin.
(www.decnv.com).

Some areas of the site were to be the home of basement car parks, which required excavation of material. As the site was formerly a gasworks since 1830, it meant that there was a lot of contamination in the soil from years of industrious use. Coal tar and spent oxides were commonly found throughout the site. It was found that the underground tanks where the coal tar was stored were sometimes badly built and therefore the tar leaked into the ground. A chemical works was also present on the site thanks to the by-products of the gasworks, this also was a source of contamination. New tanks installed since the 1960's also caused leakages of Petrol, Naptha and distillate spirit (Brown at al, 2006).

The geology of the site was very similar to the Cork docklands. A fill layer which was found to be heavily contaminated, followed by bolder clay, sands and gravels and a limestone bedrock. The contamination penetrated the sands and gravels in parts and mobile PAH's were commonly found (Brown at al, 2006).

A quantified risk assessment was undertaken at preliminary stages to assess the risk of contamination to human health and the surrounding environment. United States EPA guidelines were the main guidelines used for this assessment.

A Hybrid Perimeter wall, made up of a slurry trench and piles was constructed six meters below the ground. The wall was to have a low permeability to prevent leakage and was to be able to resist shear. Removal of contaminated soil to landfill (dig and dump) was not an option as there was no facility available in Ireland. Bioremediation would take too long for the required timescale of development and Thermal Desorption was considered too expensive. Soil washing was considered to be the best treatment as the particles in the fill were big enough to be effectively washed. An Environmental Management System was submitted to the EPA before any waste activities took place (Brown at al, 2006).

Soil was assessed using chemical analysis, the site was broken up into 20m x 10m x 1m cells for assessment. Groundwater and emissions in the site were monitored before and after remediation. Gravel washing and vibration screening was done on site and the physio-chemical washing was done off site. The water from the process was moved to an on site water treatment plant.

Soil was shipped to Antwerp in Belgium for soilwashing and to Rotterdam in Holland for Thermal Desorption. The EPA state that under the two licenses, that 160,000 tonnes of hazardous material was exported to landfill and 114,000 tonnes of non-hazardous waste was exported to landfill (Motherway, 2009).

6.2.2 Former Waterford Crystal Car Park, Kingsmeadow, Waterford.

This is a 1.1 hectare development including a leisure centre, swimming pool, warehouse, retail outlets, supermarket, offices and a car park facility. In 2003 contamination was found after planning was granted. The EPA revealed that the contamination was from oil, this would have damaging consequences for the concrete and therefore had to be removed. In 2008 the planning was granted but first the oil contamination had to be dealt with through the satisfaction of the EPA and the Local Authority.

6.3 Remediation in the U.K.

6.3.1 The UK's Brownfield Sites.

The UK has a long industrial past and with this comes a lot of old industrial sites. As time progressed, these sites have to be redeveloped to suit modern needs. A lot of contamination is found in the soil in these sites. In recent times the public have become very environmentally aware and standards of environmental protection and human health have become more important. This has fed into the legislation and guidelines for dealing with contaminated soil. The UK has a much longer history of dealing with Brownfield sites and is therefore perhaps a model for Ireland to follow as it begins to draw up its own guidelines in respect to the topic. In England and Wales alone there is said to be 325,000 sites/ 300,000 hectares of contaminated land (Environment Agency, 2008).

6.3.2 United Kingdom Best Practice.

The UK has evolved in its development to remediate soil. Before much of the contaminated soil was sent to landfill but now much more is being treated on site, thanks to government incentives and a move towards sustainable treatment where the soil can be reused on site afterwards.

The Environmental Protection Act, 1990 deals with contaminated land in England. Scotland and Wales introduced similar regimes in 2000 and 2001 (Burden, 2009). Northern Ireland does not yet have an official regime for contaminated land. The UK follows their own assessments and guidelines, such as those outlined by the department of the environment, food and rural affairs (Defra) and the Clea model. The application of risk assessment follows that of the Source to Pathway to Receptor approach, where one of these is gotten rid of, i.e. break pathway or remove the source or receptor. Conceptual site models are used to gain an insight of the contamination and to conclude a good measure to break the source/ pathway/ receptor link. From speaking to one company in the UK called VertaseFLI, we learned that "of the 500,000 tonnes of contaminated soil dealt with in 2008, only 20,000 tonnes of that were sent to landfill". This represents the shift in thinking in the UK to more sustainable remediation.

Redevelopment of contaminated land is encouraged more in Britain than urban sprawl onto Greenfield sites. Fig 6.4 below represents the amount of new dwellings built on Brownfield and Greenfield sites in England. Currently in the UK 60% of new homes are to be built on Brownfield sites (Dottridge, 2009). However the National Brownfield Strategy does recognise that not all Brownfield sites are suitable for redevelopment.

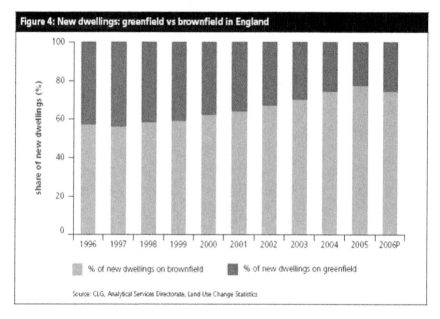

Source: CLG, Analytical Services Directorate, Land Use Change Statistics

Fig 6.4 New Dwellings Built on Greenfield and Brownfield in England. (www.landbanking.us).

6.4 United Kingdom Soil Remediation Case Studies.

6.4.1 Cannock, Pritchard Developments, Former Automotive Lighting Factory.

This site is a former automotive factory and is therefore similar to the Ford Distribution centre in Cork where the Atlantic Quarter is due to be built. The facility in Cannock, Staffordshire was to be transformed to a housing estate. The operation which was worth £1,000,000 took 42 weeks.

On the site, a large effluent treatment plant had to be decommissioned as well as the general demolition of the site. Large underground structures were to be removed and crushed for reuse along with other concrete debris.

Methods of treatment included Ex-situ Bioremediation, three in-situ treatments for removal of Chlorinated solvents and TCE (Piddington, 2009).Air Sparging and Vapour Recovery were used to enhance bio degradation and remediate the groundwater. Wells for air sparging were dug and an onsite treatment plant for the vapours set up, connected to the wells through pipes.

6.4.2 Former Tar and Chemical Works, Cadishead, Manchester.

In a site of 65,000m2 with 120,000m3 of contaminated soil, the cleanup of the former tar and chemical works in Cadishead was no small undertaking. This site is to be developed into a residential area with 380 homes, because of this it had to be ensured that there would be no risk to the population that would move in there. The contaminants included oils, Diesel, BTEX, Phenol, Tar and Naphthalene which were found in a fill layer of made ground over alluvial Silts. The clean up was valued at £3,200,000 (Piddington, 2009).

A major cause of the contamination spread throughout the site was that the groundwater was very shallow and was able to move freely in the fill material. In fact even the deep groundwater over 5m below was contaminated with Phenols, Naphthalene and BTEX. The whole site was completely contaminated above safety levels.

The project which was undertaken by VertaseFLI, followed the following strategy.
The Demolition material was reused on site for fill etc., all effluent was recovered from underground structures, Dewatering of perched effluent table, contaminated soil was excavated, and on-site treatment used where possible, material was divided for the various treatments such as ex-situ vapour recovery and oxidation, biological treatments and off site disposal, remediation of groundwater, install capillary break layer to allow for the clean cover layer, get site ready for housing (Piddington, 2009).

This strategy was broken up into phases and ultimately took 70 weeks. Three in-situ systems were installed to remediate deep groundwater. Fig 6.5 shows one of ex-situ biological treatment beds used for remediation of soils affected by hydrocarbon contamination. It is important for contractors like VertaseFLI to excavate selectively therefore reducing costs and saving time.

Fig 6.5 Ex-situ Biological Treatment Bed.
(www.vertase.co.uk).

7.0 Remediation Solutions.

Many treatments are available to remediate soil. This chapter explains the process of some of the main treatments which are relevant to the Cork South Docklands. It outlines the advantages and disadvantages of each treatment. Included in this chapter are important points on monitoring the environment during and after remediation. The construction phase of a project with respect to the remediation process is also discussed.

7.1 Choosing a Suitable Solution.

When faced with a soil contamination project, it is vital that a good site investigation is completed as this helps identify what treatment is necessary and where it is necessary. When the contaminants are identified, appropriate treatment option may also be identified. The design of the building is an important aspect to be accounted for to help choose the best option. Developments tend to have different types of priorities, such as the time, costs, or even stipulations by planners, environmental agencies etc. This will ultimately dictate the method of soil and groundwater remediation.

The remediation solution can be as simple as containing the contaminated soil, covering it over, dumping in landfill or a range of more technical treatments to get rid of the problem completely. However, when choosing a solution, the countries legislation can be a powerful decision maker, in that it may dictate what to do with certain waste or forbid certain practices, such as containment. A site's location is another important factor in choosing a solution. For example if there is no free space on site, bringing in mobile treatment plants may not be an option. A location factor in Cork's south docklands is that there is an option to use the river as a means of transport for excavated soil. When all these factors are considered it is easier consider the best solution on offer. In most scenarios it is important to note that there is no single treatment which can deal with all the contaminants and therefore it is a mix and match of many treatments that tends to be the most effective approach. All treatments have their advantages and disadvantages, which will be outlined in this chapter.

7.2 Possible Solutions.

7.2.1 Dig and Dump.

Dig and Dump is the name given to the process of excavation contaminated soil and simply taking it to a landfill. It is a very simple method of getting rid of the problem from the site. Dig and Dump until recently was also quiet cheap as opposed to other remediation options. With the addition of new legislation such as waste and landfill directives, it is no longer possible to mix hazardous and non- hazardous soil in landfills. There is no facility in Ireland for the disposal of hazardous waste, therefore to use this process for the South Docklands we could only send non hazardous waste to landfill with less than 10PAH's > 40mg/kg. The rest would have to be exported.

The Landfill Directive was fully implemented across the European Union on the 16th of July 2004 and dictated that there was to be no co-disposal of hazardous and non-hazardous waste, that hazardous waste had to be pre treated and basic characterisation of the waste should be done comparing it to the Waste Acceptance Criteria. (Elliott, 2004). This has increased the cost of Dig and Dump and therefore it is no longer an attractive option. In the UK some landfill sites charge up to £200 per tonne to accept contaminated soil (The Concrete Centre, 2007), these extortionate costs have effectively reduced the quantities of contaminated soil going to landfill and encouraged the use of remediation technologies.

Dig and dump is seen as an unsavoury option by the environmental protection campaigners because the contaminated soil is not treated, it is just moved to another location.

The advantages of dig and dump include:
- It is a simple low tech operation.
- Once the soil is moved to landfill, it is no longer the responsibility of the site owner.
- Does not require a permit in Ireland.

- There is no need to monitor the soil after its removal as there is for other treatments

Disadvantages:

- High transport cost.
- No site in Ireland for Hazardous material.
- High waste production.
- Expensive.
- Must use licenses contractor.
- Not a sustainable solution.

7.2.2 Containment, Cover and Permeable Reactive Barriers.

Containment is where the contaminated soil is contained in the ground, usually by a concrete (slurry) perimeter wall which reaches down to a considerable depth. This is then covered by a cover system which is often a layer of clay capping or other soil capping to a certain depth. This method is effectively trying to cut off the contaminated soil from any receptors, but this is very hard to do as there is a risk of penetration into the aquifers. Perimeter walls should have low permeability to reduce spread of contamination. This is not a sustainable solution because the contamination is not being treated.

Using Permeable Reactive Barriers is a new sustainable technology used to remedy the problem with containment. This is where a reactive zone is put in place as part of the barrier around the contaminated area (see fig 7.1). The idea is for the groundwater, directed by the barrier walls to flow to a point of treatment and enter gates of reactive material where it is treated and then flows out. This is a passive process but takes many years to completely remediate the soil.

These treatments are possible for Cork Docklands, however in areas of shallow aquifers, Permeable Reactive Barriers may not be very effective. PRB's are not very suitable where developers want a quick solution .

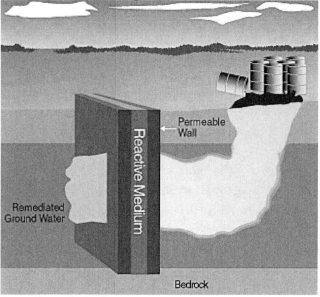

Permeable reactive barriers have the potential to lower the cost and increase the effectiveness of groundwater cleanup.

Fig 7.1 Schematic of a Permeable Reactive Barrier. (www.p2pays.org)

Advantages:
- If using permeable reactive barriers, it is sustainable.
- Not as expensive as other treatments.
- Low maintenance.

Disadvantages:
- Takes 10 – 30 years.
- Not very suitable for development land.
- Decommissioning the PRB.

7.2.3 Pump and Treat.

Pump and Treat is used to remediate groundwater. Firstly the excavation should be dewatered and that water treated, perhaps by a mobile treatment plant. Then boreholes are driven and trenches can be installed to bring the water to a pumping area. This is then treated. This process should continue until the extracted water is below contamination levels. The cleaned water is then discharged and re-injected. The problem with this is there should be perimeter walls installed to prevent fresh uncontaminated water being dragged in to replace the pumped water. The mobile water treatment facility must be adapted to the different contaminants found in sites.

Advantages:
- Water is cleaned and re injected
- No major excavation required except boreholes
- Treatment of water reduces risk of contamination spread

Disadvantages:
- Needs constant pumping.
- Takes a long time.
- Slow and possibly not very effective as a treatment on its own.

7.2.4 Stabilisation/ Solidification (s/s).

Stabilisation/ Solidification also known as soil mixing, is where contaminants are stabilised by being immobilised but are not reduced. The soil is stabilised using chemicals (reagent) or physically by mixing with a matrix such as cement. It is suitable for almost all contaminants and does not require much disruption on site. Developers can quickly get on with their work. However the contaminants are not removed, just frozen. Reagent which are used as binders, can be quite complex and may be different for different types of contaminants.

Advantages:
- Quick solution for remediation.
- Low disturbance.
- Little excavation necessary.
- Relatively cheap

Disadvantages:
- Does not get rid of contaminants, only cuts path to receptor.
- Alters soil characteristics.
- Concern about the durability of the treatment.
- Possible harmful by- products.

7.2.5 Bioremediation with Air Sparging.

Bioremediation is where microbes are put into the contaminated soil to naturally breakdown contaminants. Water and Carbon Dioxide can be added to speed up the process. Bioremediation can be used in conjunction with air sparging. Here air is blown into the groundwater or underlying aquifer and the contaminants move up the soil and are extracted by vapour extraction pumps. This combined system is very effective but is not suitable for hydrocarbons associated with coal tar found in gasworks and is a slow process (Brown, 2006). This process is used for Volatile chlorinated hydrocarbons as well as other contaminants. Another type of bioremediation is Phytoremediation, where plants are used to remove contaminants. This however would not be suitable where livestock are involved.

Advantages:
- Cheap when excavation is not an option.
- Treats groundwater and soil simultaneously.
- Does not require excavation
- Sustainable.

Disadvantages:
- Only suitable for some contaminants.
- Slow process
- Air pollution licence needed for air sparging emissions

7.2.6 Thermal Desorption.

With thermal desorption soil is excavated and put into a furnace where contaminants are burned. The emissions are then treated to an adequate level. Ireland does not have a facility for thermal desorption. We would have to transport the soil. It is a very expensive method of treatment. There are two types of apparatus for desorption, a thermal screw and a rotary dryer. Water should be added to increase the moisture content of the soil after the process. The soil however is normally not fit for ecological activity after treatment. Fig 7.2 below outlines the processes of thermal desorption. When compared to incineration, thermal desorption proves operates at a lower temperature, it therefore proves cheaper. The soil can still be sold and the emissions are not as bad as those from incineration.

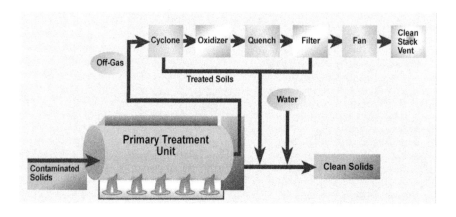

Fig 7.2 Flow Diagram for Thermal Desorption.
(http://groundwaterprogram.army.mil)

Advantages:
- Capable of treating contaminants that soil washing cannot.
- Effective remediation process
- Can choose between High and Low Desortion.

Disadvantages:
- High cost.
- High Carbon Dioxide output.
- Need to treat emissions.
- Can destroy soil.

7.2.7 Soil Washing

Soil washing works best on gravel soils. Soil is extracted from the ground and brought to a soil washing facility, usually on site such as the one in Fig 7.3. The aim is to separate the contaminants from the soil. Gravel washing helps separate soil grading, here gravel is moved through a rotating drum where it is washed with high pressure water jets. Contaminants are more likely to absorb into clay soils, these will be present in the fines after soil washing. The mixture is left settle and the water sent to a water treatment plant. The soil washing process does not get rid of contaminants or immobilise them, but it does bring to contaminants to a concentrated point, mainly in the fines strata. This soil which is concentrated with contaminants should be disposed of and the rest reused in the development.

Soil washing is a good method to use as part of a bigger remediation process but it is not very sustainable solution on its own. It is important to test the soil after soil washing to determine its capability of being reused.

Advantages:
- Can be done on site.
- Cheaper than many other methods.
- Minimises waste material because it massively reduces amount of contaminated material.
- Removes most soil contaminants.
- Separates soil into its different sizes.
- Relatively quick process.

Disadvantages:
- Water must be treated.
- Concentrated soil must be treated by another process or taken to landfill.
- Waste licence required.
- Soil must be excavated
- Not very suitable for clay and silt soil.
- High energy requirement.

Fig 7.3 On Site Soil Washing Plant. (www.oilpoll.com)

Most of the above methods are suitable for the Cork South Docklands, whether they are used in conjunction with another method or not.

7.3 During and After Remediation.

7.3.1 Monitoring.

Once a remediation process is chosen it is important to monitor progress. This gives an idea of the effectiveness of the process and when it will be completed. Correct monitoring can also give an indication of whether the contaminants are spreading. During remediation emissions should also be monitored such as vapours, dust, noise and odours. Groundwater should also be monitored as it is an indication of the spread of contamination into an aquifer.

7.3.2 Construction Phase.

In the construction phase of a development, it is vital that whatever remediation that is or has taken place is not disturbed. For example if piles were driven into the aquifer they could carry contaminants. In general it is important to reduce any pollution impact on soil, surface water and groundwater during construction. This was recognized by The Construction Industry Research and Information Association (C.I.R.I.A.), when they issued guidelines for the "control of water pollution from construction sites". This includes relevant protection measures during construction activities, such as emergency response plans, education employees of prevention measures, spill control equipment, dedicated refuelling locations with adequate storage tanks and drip trays, controlled site drainage and more, (Masters-Williams et al, 2001).

For basements it is proposed to take retaining walls into low permeability soil or where they are not available to construct cut off walls thereby reducing the flow rates of water into the excavation. Measures must be taken during construction to minimise movement or collapse of an excavations walls. Regular monitoring of wells and other groundwater should take place.

Once construction is complete, monitoring the sites remediation status should still take place for a while to ensure a healthy soil and groundwater status is attained.

8.0 The Future of Remediation.

The future of remediation is rather different from its past. In this chapter new soil remediation standards and developments are discussed.

8.1 The Future?

Brownfield remediation is not going to go away any time soon. Countries populations are rising and urban areas are trying to cope with these growing numbers. There is a need for the containment of urban sprawl to protect rural areas and wildlife. This combined with the need to redevelop dilapidated urban areas fuels the necessity to develop Brownfield sites. Environmental agencies and health authorities from the EU and governments encourage remediation of contaminated sites to protect people and the environment.

One example of large scale development on sites that are currently contaminated, is the Olympic village in Stratford, London for the 2012 Olympics, (See Fig 8.1). It is set to be one of the largest remediated sites in the UK

Fig 8.1 Stratford, London Olympic Site.
(www.propertyinvesting.net).

New technologies are coming in stream all the time as science is progressing. The ultimate aim would be to have very fast acting and cheap in-situ treatments as this would prove the least costly and least hindrance to developers.

Directives like the one in the UK, to build 60% new houses on Brownfield are very necessary as they encourage the development of disadvantaged and idle areas. In the future it would not be surprising to see more and more directives like this introduced into countries.

In the E.U. in 2006 there was an estimated 3.5 million potentially contaminated sites (Haemers, 2008). This is massive market for remediation companies and should ensure a lot of work in the future in this industry.

If Ireland is to move on in the future and catch up with global best practice, we will have to make licenses easier to attain so mobile treatment plants can be set up. We will also have to encourage and educate developers and planners on Brownfield sites and the advantages of their remediation. Appropriate and adequate legislation should be drawn up and an official risk assessment should be utilized.

8.2 Sustainable Remediation.

Sustainable development has been defined as follows;

"Sustainable development is development that meets the needs of the present without compromising the ability of future generations to meet their own needs" (Brundtland, 1987).

Sustainable remediation is the preferred way of the future. It reduces the amount of waste soil going into land fill by treating it and reusing it on site and therefore reduces the particular countries carbon footprint. Sustainable remediation also reduces the impact on ecosystems and the environment in the future.

Although sustainable remediation can be expensive, in the long run it is worth it because one has a reassurance that the remediated land has a clean bill of health and that the aquifers will not be contaminated, thereby protecting the users of the land from illness, nasty odours and other negative effects. Also a peace of mind is given about the foundations, in that they will not be attacked by chemicals and that stability is reassured due to the knowledge of ground conditions instead of relying on previous fill a new fill layer can be laid.

The Cork City Council policy states that, the remediation proposals for The Cork Docklands are to be sustainable, (Coughlan et al, 2009).

8.3 Green Remediation.

Green remediation considers all the environmental effects of the remediation process and the long term effect. It favours sustainable treatments. Currently in the United States, green remediation is being developed by the Environmental Protection Agency. Along with the use of best practice techniques, they seek to reduce the energy needed by the treatment process, reduce air emissions, protect the water and reduce water usage, consider and protect the impacts to the ecosystem, reduce waste and material consumption and finally consider the long term action required (BrownfieldsTSC, 2008).

Green remediation strives to go to great lengths to conserve energy. The use of renewable energies and environmentally friendly fuels help in the supply of green power for remediation. Grants are being granted to fund some projects in the States as an incentive to Green development. Green Remediation favours low energy, passive treatments such as Bioremediation, Phytoremediation, Permeable Reactive barriers, cover systems and Monitored Natural Attenuation, which is essentially a monitored, "do nothing scenario" suitable for sites with little risk of contamination migration.

The United Sates may be leading the field in Green remediation but it is only a matter of time before the rest of the developed world follows suit. Hopefully the Cork Docklands will take the opportunity to showcase Green remediation in Ireland.

9.0 Conclusions.

The following chapter will discuss the various conclusions from our research.

9.1 Scale of the Project.

The Cork Docklands is a massive undertaking that will transform the city and a positive step for Cork City to develop its local economy and put more life into the heart of the City. From the findings of reports such as those in chapter 3, it is clear that soil contamination in the South Docklands is a substantial issue. However it must be remembered that not all the soil in the docklands is contaminated, and of the soil which is contaminated, only some of it is sufficiently contaminated to pose a threat to human health and the surrounding environment.

To find out the level of contamination, a site should undergo an investigation by qualified personnel. The investigation should include a risk assessment of the contaminants which takes into account the proposed development type and all possible links from contaminated ground to potential receptors. With the information from these reports, the best solution can be sought, while taking into account the most economical and environmentally friendly options.

9.2 Current Remediation Practice

In Ireland there are no best practice guidelines. Soil Remediation is not a very developed field in Ireland. We have undertaken very few large remediation projects. There are very few remediation contractors in Ireland compared with the U.K. For the Cork South Docklands there is a freedom to choose whatever remediation procedure is required and little legislation restraints. Ireland exports far too much soil as waste to foreign countries. This adds to our carbon footprint and also does not look good from a recycling point of view. Developments in Ireland in recent years have largely been located on Greenfield sites because our infrastructure and residential buildings were catching up with a growing population and economic boom. Of the projects which were developed on Brownfield, only a fraction of these would have been contaminated.

The U.K. United States and some European countries are ahead of Ireland with their developments in and standards for Remediation. More rigorous legislation and availability of remediation procedures mean that they tend to use sustainable methods. The amount of Brownfield material going to landfill is significantly reduced in these countries.

9.3 Legislation and Guidelines

Currently in Ireland there is no legislation for dealing with suspected contaminated land. As a result of this there is no statutory definition of contaminated land nor any person, authority or agency identified as having the responsibility to identify contaminated land. The basis for the identification of contaminated land in the UK is the statutory definition in Part IIA of the Environmental Protection Act 1990. This Act also establishes who is responsible for the identification of contaminated land, how it should be identified, who is responsible for the clean up and defines what remediation is.

As it stands at present Irish legislation does not apply to contaminated land unless the polluted soil is categorised as waste. This applies to both soil excavated and left in situ at present but by 2010 the new Waste Framework Directive will be fully introduced. The introduction of this will result in contaminated soil left in situ no longer being classified as waste and therefore not within the remit of Irish legislation.

Presently in Ireland if a landowner or developer suspects land to be contaminated there is no specific legislation or guidelines for them to follow. The landowner or developer is the person or organisation that must identify the site as being contaminated and it is up to them to liaise with local authority regarding the action to be taken. The local authority may be able to provide information on the site history and may indicate areas of concern which should be included in a site investigation but different local authorities will have varying levels of knowledge and experience in terms of dealing with contaminated land.

In short, without a national standard the onus is on the landowner or developer to develop a procedure for dealing with the identification and remediation by seeking information from where they can; local authority, the Environmental Protection Agency or a suitably qualified consultant.

9.4 Human Health (and environmental) Risk

Risk assessment of human health and environmental risk in Ireland tends to be a very simplified approach. The general practice is the use of source pathway receptor linkages and a conceptual model. As there are no guidelines in Ireland the conceptual model is often very simplified.

Within the South Docklands the most widely contaminated area is the fill layer, where levels of the contaminant are above the Dutch Intervention Value risk to human health is a concern. As the pathway is generally through direct contact the risk is only a concern for developments involving gardens and other outdoor features. The two contaminants found that are at greatest risk to human health are vinyl chloride and 1,2-dichloroethene. In areas where both fill and clay are contaminated with vinyl chloride and 1,2-dichloroethene contamination there is a risk of liver damage, cancer and neurological symptoms where high exposure levels exist or if exposed over a long period of time. This may occur if the source pathway receptor linkage is completed through the contaminants reaching the groundwater or the contaminated area or from inhalation. The environmental risks found in the South Docklands were due to lead and copper present in the top 1 metre above ground level, if this soil remains in situ it has the may result in ecological problems.

9.5 Remediation Solutions

The older remediation techniques of Dig and Dump, is not seen as good options anymore. With Dig and Dump all material which leaves the site is considered waste and a waste licence is required. Other techniques successfully contain contamination but do not fix the problem. Covering and stabilization / solidification are examples of this. While they do have their advantages, they are not sustainable.

Using a mix of treatments is the best option for remediation. This helps eliminate all of the contaminants on a site if the appropriate treatments are picked. Bioremediation with air sparging and permeable reactive barriers offer more sustainable solution. They can also treat the soil without hindering developments.

10.0 Recommendations

These are our recommendations for the remediation of the Cork South Docklands. We will also recommend suitable legislation, guidelines and best practice which we think should be introduced in Ireland for the future.

10.1 Recommendations for the future of Remediation in Ireland

10.1.1 Legislation and Guidelines

The first step in moving forward with the legislative vacuum that is associated with contaminated land in Ireland is by establishing a statutory definition. This definition may be derived from examining other definitions of contaminated land such as that in use in the UK. A suggestion of for a definition is as follows; 'Contaminated land is any land, which when sufficient concentrations of a substance are present in, on or under the land, there is a risk of harm to human health or the environment'.

We also propose that a legal standard for the dealing with contaminated land be produced for Ireland based on the statutory definition. It should state the definition of contaminated land, outline the process for identifying that a site is contaminated, identify the person or organisation eligibility for the remediation of the waste and assign an obligation on this person to submit a report of proposed remediation options for approval by the local authority. The standard should also give the local authority the permission to visit sites to perform spot checks that the remediation process is being carried out as stated in the approved report.

Another recommended introduction to legislation is in relation to exportation of contaminated soil. Where possible exportation of soil should be prevented, it's not particularly ethical to off load our problems o another country. Where possible we should treat our contaminated soils within Ireland. We recommend that the local authority should set a restriction on the maximum quantity of contaminated soil which can be exported, before the developer must legally investigate the possibility of on site treatment of the soil.

At present it is during the planning process with Cork County Council that land contamination is dealt with. Within the planning application an Environmental Impact Statements (EIS) is presented for the site. We proposed that more detail of the consideration and investigation of contaminated soil and groundwater should be included. Such as although disposal may be the proposed remedial action, identify why this was chosen. Show that a more sustainable approach was first considered and explain why disposal was chosen as the most suitable method. This will show the developer has due regard for the significance of contaminated land and the consequences which may result.

10.1.2 Risk Assessment

In Ireland, the Environmental Protection Agency (EPA) is not just involved in licensing and monitoring; it also promotes environmentally sound practices and publishes guidance. For this reason we propose that the EPA compile a document outlining risk assessment methods as there no established methodology for the identification of human health and environmental risk in Ireland. This would give developers a clear view of the steps to be carried out in assessing the risks present. The document would first outline the information needed to compile the assessment (obtain from a site investigation) and then give guidance as to how to produce a conceptual model and how to identify source pathway receptor linkages.

10.1.3 Improve Capacity to Deal With Remediation Internally.

Ireland needs to increase its capacity to deal with contaminated land. We must introduce specialised facilities for Thermal Desorption and perhaps develop facilities where soil can be taken to for bioremediation. However onsite treatment is the best option if possible, it reduces costs and waste. For onsite treatment to develop in Ireland we need a quick and lenient licensing procedure for mobile treatments plants. This would allow onsite soil-washing, thermal desorption and pump and treat plants to be easily set up without too much delay. This was one reason for exporting a lot of soil for treatment on the Sir John Rogerson's Quay site in Dublin. The government could give sponsorship to a central facility in Ireland to clean soil. The government could also set up a forum to improve and develop internal remediation.

10.1.5 Sustainable and Green Remediation

Sustainable remediation is the way of the future, there is no point in burying or freezing a contamination problem which could be a risk in the future. The financial burden of remediation can be high, which sometimes means that sustainable remediation is not an option, however sustainable remediation may not have to be as expensive as it may seem. Bioremediation with air sparging is one of the best sustainable treatments around. It can be done in-situ and poses little interruption to the development. Bacteria can be introduced to the soil and aquifer, with the only maintenance factor being the vapours or pumped out groundwater. Small wind turbines can be used to power the vapour and water pumps which should reduce the cost of long term pumping.

Green remediation showcases could be brought to Ireland. They could educate us on how we could minimise waste and the environmental effect of remediation processes Legislation and incentives for utilising green and sustainable remediation would greatly increase their prominence in the sector

10.1.6 Encourage Remediation

To help reduce Brownfield sites, encouragement should be given to developer. Tax incentives for Brownfield developments or directives towards big developers to build on a certain % of Brownfield sites are two such options. Annual awards could be given to excellent remediation projects, which would increase a company's profile. Another incentive would be the issuing of grants from the government or Sustainable Energy Ireland (S.E.I.) who could send out trained advisors to developers for guidance. A more risky option would be to supply a guaranteed mortgage to developers of Brownfield sites

10.1.7 Raise Awareness of the positives of Brownfield Remediation.

The advantages of raising awareness of remediation are as follows
- It helps achieve greater co-operation during a development from all involved on the project and nearby residents
- Reduces the risk of lowered house prices, as people can trust the site is clean.
- Allows government grants to be given to sustainable remediation without a public grudge

10.2 Recommendations for the Cork docklands

What we recommended for the future of remediation in Ireland (in 10.1), we also recommend for the Cork Docklands Project. Nevertheless, this section outlines more of our recommendations, which are specifically relevant to The Cork South Docklands.

10.2.1 Detailed Site Specific Site Investigation.

For the Cork South Docklands, We recommend that more detailed, site specific soil and groundwater investigations be undertaken. T.J. O' Connor's report on the "South Docklands Contamination Study" is a very good general guideline for the areas which are intensively contaminated, however it is not sufficient for a site by site basis. It is important for site owners and developers to be aware and responsible for the level of contamination on their sites. The onus should be on the developer to undertake a detailed site investigation, this should be stipulated as part of the conditions for the granting of planning permission.

This gives a better case by case view of the contamination level. Therefore the risk assessment of the contamination can be assessed better than if one were to rely on a general site investigation of the docklands.

10.2.2 What Should be Treated?

We recommend that heavily contaminated areas of contamination are to be treated, where soil is found to have values greater than the Dutch Intervention Values for VCH's and PAH's Lead and other harmful substances and areas where the aquifer is being infiltrated by contaminants. Significant sources of contamination should also be treated to reduce spread. If some contaminated zones do not pose any threat to the human health or the ecosystem then they do not have to be remediated thereby reducing costs and unnecessary interruption of the soil. However it should be ensured that all the end users of the sites should not have any link to contaminated soil or groundwater. Also areas where a buildings structure would be at risk from corrosion due to contaminants found should be remediated. Groundwater, especially in aquifers, should be clean and healthy. Any groundwater which is not should be treated.

When all dangerous contaminants are looked after, further remediation for any particular site should depend on its end use. Green areas such as gardens and parks should be remediated to a high standard. Office blocks on the other hand, where there is low level contamination could simply cover the site with a shallow veneer of new soil.

For sustainable remediation we would recommend that no possibly risky contaminant be left untreated, and that any low level, minimum risk areas should also be treated if they cannot remediate themselves naturally within the next 10 to15 years.

10.2.3 Recommended Method of Treatment for the Cork South Docklands

We recommend in-situ sustainable treatments if possible, with bioremediation and air sparging being the dominant method of remediation. The only waste should be that from Thermal Desorption, this should be capable of being dumped in our landfills but no other waste should need to go to landfill. Soil-washing should be used to minimise waste and Thermal Desorption to destroy hazardous contaminants from the soil washing process. If there was found to be significant co-operation between developers, a centralised, shared facility could be set up in the Docklands to provide remediation treatments such as soil washing, Thermal Desorption and ex-situ Bioremediation beds. Mobile treatment plants for water and vapour extraction plants should be confined to the area of remediation. Sites should recycle as much soil and rubble as possible.

Groundwater containing contaminants should be pumped and treated in conjunction with bioremediation, to ensure that all the aquifers are made healthy. Areas with little or no clean protective layers between groundwater level and ground level should be remediated and a more substantial protective layer put in place, e.g. Hall's Port Quarter site.

Volatile chlorinated hydrocarbons (VCH's) are the most dangerous contaminants found in the docklands. We recommend Soil washing of the fill and clay layer and Thermal Desorption.

Permeable reactive barriers may be a good idea for certain scenarios but are better avoided so there is no need for decommissioning in years to come should a development arise.

All emissions should be monitored and made safe during remediation treatments. Monitoring should also continue on remediated sites and aquifers to ensure successful completion of the task.

10.2.4 Other Recommendations

Remediation procedures should be well planned out and carried out with the co-operation of their adjacent sites to ensure all contamination which needs to be removed is removed. Traffic management and facility use should be coordinated to produce a smooth system within the South Docklands site.

Sustainability should be a priority as we keep in mind the possibility of future developments. Waste should be kept to a minimum with recycling of materials a priority. Green remediation should be attempted on some site with local government support to increase awareness of its existence.

Cork City Council should provide incentives to developers to reduce waste and introduce legislation on sustainable remediation of the site. They should also provide remediation advisors to developers and inspectors to assess proper remediation while all the time keeping in consultation with the Environmental Protection Agency.

REFERENCES:

Archiseek.com,
Available from:
http://www.archiseek.com/content/showthread.php?p=64487
(Assessed 24th March 2009)

Association for Organics Recycling, (2008) "Revised Waste
Framework Directive"
Available from:

http://www.organics-recycling.org.uk/index.php?option=com_content&view=article&id=255%3Arevised-waste-framework-directive&catid=1%3Alatest-news&Itemid=18&showall=1, 19 (Accessed 10th April 2009)

Brown T, Crowther J (2006), "REMEDIATION OF THE FORMER GASWORKS SITE AT SIR JOHN ROGERSON'S QUAY, DUBLIN", January 2006.

Bruntland Commission, (1987), "Our Common Future", 1987,

Burden L, (2009), "HUMAN HEALTH RISK ASSESSMENT AND ITS ROLE IN BROWNFIELD REDEVELOPMENT", RPS group, Engineers Ireland Seminar 2009, March 2009.

Coghlan S, Walsh G (2009), "Brownfield Regeneration, Cork Docklands Challenges", Engineers Ireland Seminar, March 2009.

Conneely P, O'Sullivan T, (2006) "Land-use Planning Advice for Cork County Council in relation to Goulding Chemicals Ltd. At Centre Park Road, Cork", 5 December 2006
Available from:
http://www.corkdocklands.ie/infrastructure/sevesosites/gouldings.pdf
(Accessed 13 February)

Cork City Council Planning Enquiry, Atlantic Quarter planning reference number 08/32919, Port Quarter planning reference number 08/33238.
Available from:
http://planenquiry.corkcity.ie/planningenquiry/MainFrames.aspx
(Accessed 15 March 2009)

Cork Docklands, (2008), "Submission of planning application T.P. Planning application T.P. 08/33238 R & H Hall – R & H Hall site, Kennedy Quay".
Available from
http://www.corkdocklands.ie/news/portquarterplanningappl ication/
(Accessed 10th March 2009).

Cork Docklands, (2008), "SEVESO Sites",
Available From:
http://www.corkdocklands.ie/infrastructure/sevesosites/
(Accessed 10th March 2009)

Cork Docklands, Cork City Council, "South Docks Local Area Plan", 2008,
Available from:
http://www.corkdocklands.ie/planning/southdockslocalarea plan/
(Accessed 14th Marc 2009)

Cox A, Spence D, (2008) "How policy considerations impact upon judge-made environmental law", Law and the Environment 2005 Third Annual Conference for Environmental Professionals, 14 April 2005
Available from:
www.ucc.ie/law/events/environ05papers/spence.doc
(Accessed 21 March 2009)

Defra, (2008) "Guidance on the Legal Definition of Contaminated Land", July 2008
Available from:
http://www.defra.gov.uk/environment/land/contaminated/p df/legal-definition.pdf
(Accessed 19 March 2009)

Decnv.com, Brownfields, "Remediation of a former gasworks in Dublin (Ireland)",
Available from:
http://www.decnv.com/EN/projects/brownfields/remediatio
n_of_a_former_gasworks_in_dublin_ireland.html?PHPSESS
ID=9d0a50752b89815d7e89508cf686fbcf
(Accessed 16th March 2009)

Dottridge J, (2 Engineers Ireland Seminar 2009, March 2009.009),"Realistic, cost effective and sustainable remediation", Mott MacDonald, Engineers Ireland Seminar 2009, March 2009.

Elliott S, (2004)," The end for dig and dump",
Available from:
http://www.edie.net/news/news_story.asp?id=10284&channe
l=0.
(Accessed 14th April 2009)

ENVA, (2008), ENVA Soil Treatment, About.
Available From:
http://soiltreatment.enva.com/About/About/Navigation.html
(Accessed 9th April 2009).

Environment Agency, 2008, "contaminated land".
Available from:
http://www.environment-
agency.gov.uk/research/library/data/34403.aspx#much.
(Accessed 9th April 2009)

Euroalert.net, (2008) "New EU waste directive will enter into force next December", Current News from the European Union
Available from:
http://euroalert.net/en/news.aspx?idn=8158

(Accessed 10 April 2009)

FinFacts, 2007, "Ireland exported 48% of its Hazardous Waste in 2006; EPA recommends treatment via incineration and landfill should be done at home".
Available from:
http://www.finfacts.com/irelandbusinessnews/publish/articl
e_1011726.shtml.
(Accessed 9th April 2009).

Forest-heath.gov.uk, (2007) "ADVICE NOTE 3 – Environmental Protection Act 1990: Part IIA Contaminated Land Regime"
Available from:
http://www.forest-heath.gov.uk/NR/rdonlyres/3C406CFC-
55D9-4BF9-A27E-
0FCA6AF22BA9/0/SEPGCLAdviceNote3.pdf
(Accessed 21 April 2009)

Groundwaterprogram.army.mil, (2004), "What is Thermal Desorption", spring 2004,
Available from:
http://groundwaterprogram.army.mil/community/facts/ther
mal_desorption.html
(Accessed 12th April 2009)

Haemers J, (2008),"Soil Remediation Market in Europe",
Available from:
http://74.125.77.132/search?q=cache:0oCAQSGM3BAJ:www.i
ntersol.fr/pdf2008/21_J%2520HAEMERS.ppt+remediATION
+MARKET&cd=2&hl=en&ct=clnk.
(Accessed 10th April 2009)

Heffernan A, (2008) "Contaminated Land" The Property Valuer, Spring 2008
Available from:

http://magico.ie/files/admin/uploads/W153_Field_2_27467.pd
f
(Accessed 28th March 2009)

Howard Holdings plc, (2008), "ATLANTIC QUARTER TO
TRANSFORM CORK CITY".
Available from:
http://www.howardholdingsplc.com/index.php/news/mor
e/atlantic-quarter-to-transform-cork-city/
(Accessed 8th March 2009).

HSE, (2003) "PADHI – HSE's Land Use Planning
Methodology"
Available from:
http://www.corkdocklands.ie/infrastructure/sevesosites/Top
az.pdf
(Accessed 13 February)

Independent.ie, (2008), "IFSC to get €1bn rival in Cork", 7th
March 2008,
Available from:
http://www.independent.ie/national-news/ifsc-to-get-
euro1bn-rival-in-cork-1308901.html
(Accessed 28th March 2009)
Landbanking.com, (2007), "Landbanking in UK", 10th October
2007,
Available from:
http://www.landbanking.us/2007/10/10/landbanking-in-uk/
(Accessed 16th April 2009)

Local Government (Water Pollution) Act 1977, (1977) "Local
authority's power to require measures to be taken to prevent
water pollution." Local Government (Water Pollution) Act
1977, Section 12, Article 1, 1977

Masters-Williams H, Heap A, (2001), "control of water pollution from construction sites, Guidance for consultants and contractors", CIRIA, 2001.

Motherway K (2009), "Contaminated Land: The Regulatory Process", Engineers Ireland Seminar 2009, March 2009.

Myhome.ie, (2009), "Planning Granted For Cork Docklands Facelift", 16th April 2009,
Available from:
http://blog.myhome.ie/post/Planning-Granted-For-Overhaul-Of-Cork-Docklands.aspx
(Accessed 18th April 2009)

O' Connor T.J. (2007), "South Docklands Contamination Study, Final Report Phase 2", July 2007

Oilpoll.com, (2008), "Specialist Waste Treatment and Recycling",
Available from:
http://www.oilpoll.com/products-technology/waste-treatment-recycling.html
(Accessed 15th April 2009)

Origin Enterprises plc(2008),"Soils, geology, surface water & groundwater", Mixed Use Development at the Hall's site, Environmental Impact Statement, Volume 1, Number 11, 2008.

Passagewestmonkstown.ie, "Cork Harbor: Haulbowline Island",
Available from:
http://www.passagewestmonkstown.ie/haulbowline-island.asp
(Accessed April 12th 2009)

Piddington C (2009), "The UK experience and its applicability to the Irish market", VertaseFLI, Engineers Ireland Seminar 2009, March 2009.

Propertyinvesting.net
Available from:
http://www.propertyinvesting.net/cgi-script/csNews/csNews.cgi?database=specialreports.db253&command=viewonex
(Accessed 20th April 2009)

P2pays.org, (1999), Initiatives Online ,"Gaining Ground on pump and treat", 1999, Vol 6,
Available from:
http://www.p2pays.org/ref/14/13983.htm
(Accessed 18th April 2009)

Sanaterre, (2009) "Shuffling towards sustainability"
Available from:
http://www.sanaterre.com/guidelines/dutch.html
(Accessed 26th March 2009)

The Concrete Centre, (2007), "On site stabilization and solidification of contaminants best option for Olympic clean-up",
Available From:
http://www.concretecentre.com/main.asp?page=1628.
(Accessed 14th April 2009)

Vertase.co.uk, Case Studies, "A Proven Track record",
Available from:

http://www.vertase.co.uk/default.asp?categoryID=6&pageID =92
(Accessed 12th April 2009)

Waste Framework Directive 2008/98/EC, (2008) "Exclusions from the scope" Waste Framework Directive 2008/98/EC, Chapter 1, Article 2 (1) (b), 2008

Waste Management Act 1996, (1996) "Waste Disposal Activities", Waste Management Act 1996 Third Schedule (3), 1996

Printed in Great Britain
by Amazon

83724542R00068